Let Freedom Ring

Betsy Ross

by Jane Duden

Consultant:
Whitney Smith, Ph.D.
Director, Flag Research Center
Winchester, Massachusetts

Bridgestone Books
an imprint of Capstone Press
Mankato, Minnesota

Bridgestone Books are published by Capstone Press
151 Good Counsel Drive • P.O. Box 669 • Mankato, Minnesota 56002
http://www.capstone-press.com

Printed in the United States of America

Library of Congress Cataloging-in-Publication Data
Duden, Jane.
      Betsy Ross / by Jane Duden.
           p. cm. — (Let freedom ring)
      Includes bibliographical references and index.
      ISBN 0-7368-1036-6
      1. Ross, Betsy, 1752–1836—Juvenile literature. 2. Revolutionaries—United States—Biography—Juvenile literature. 3. United States—History—Revolution, 1775–1783—Flags—Juvenile literature. 4. Flags—United States—History—18th century—Juvenile literature. [1. Ross, Betsy, 1752–1836. 2. Revolutionaries. 3. United States—History—Revolution, 1775–1783. 4. Flags. 5. Women—Biography.] I. Title. II. Series.
      E302.6.R77 D83 2002
      973.3´092—dc21   2001000723
                                                               CIP

Summary: Looks at the life of Betsy Ross from her Quaker childhood to her role in the Revolutionary War and her days as an independent businesswoman. Examines the legend of the Betsy Ross Flag and explains the importance of the Betsy Ross legacy in today's society.

Editorial Credits
Rebecca Aldridge, editor; Kia Bielke, designer; Stacey Field, production designer, Deirdre Barton, photo researcher

Photo Credits
J.L.G. Ferris/Wood River Gallery/PictureQuest, cover; John Ward Dunsmore/Wood River Gallery/PictureQuest, 5; Corbis, 7; Foulsham and Banfield/Hulton/Archive Photos, 8; Gloucester County Historical Society, 11; Sewcollect@aol.com, 12; Stockbyte, 13; Christ Church of Pennsylvania, 14; Compliments of Darlene Hogue, Newark, Ohio, 15; Library of Congress, 16; Martin Rodgers/stock, Boston/PictureQuest, 16; Archive Photos, 19, 29; Ewing Galloway/Index Stock, 21; Northwind Picture Archives, 25, 42; Bingham/Wood River Gallery/PictureQuest, 27; Lee Snider/Corbis, 33; The Library Company of Philadelphia, 35, 39; Alan Briere Photography, 37; Delaware River Port Authority of Pennsylvania and New Jersey, 40.

1   2   3   4   5   6   07   06   05   04   03   02

Table of Contents

Chapter One

A Quaker Childhood

Betsy Ross was a Revolutionary War Patriot who made flags that united the colonies. According to Betsy's family, George Washington asked her to sew the first Stars and Stripes in 1776. Her family said Betsy told them this story. In 1870, her grandson made a speech about the tale. Betsy's flag story quickly became an American legend.

However, Betsy's story did not surface until long after the events described, raising doubts about its accuracy. It was too late to get firsthand information. Still, Betsy's life is rich with real contributions to the American cause. Here is the story of a courageous woman and a loyal Patriot.

George Washington may have asked Betsy Ross to sew the nation's first flag.

A Quaker Family

Elizabeth Griscom was born January 1, 1752. She was the seventh of 17 children born to Samuel and Rebecca Griscom. Betsy, as everyone called Elizabeth, was born on a farm in West Jersey, Pennsylvania. Her family moved to Philadelphia two years later.

The Griscoms made room for other family members in their home. Of these, Betsy especially loved her elderly Great Aunt Sarah. This independent and spirited lady taught Betsy all about needlework. They both loved to sew and had minds of their own. Great Aunt Sarah had even run her own business. This was unusual in a time when men often were the business owners.

Many of the Griscom men had been successful carpenters. Betsy's father, Samuel, helped build the bell tower at the Philadelphia State House in Philadelphia. This building now is known as Independence Hall.

Betsy's mother was a member of a successful Quaker merchant family. The Griscoms also were Quakers, a group known as the Religious Society of Friends. Quakers were peaceful people who lived simple lives. They were against war and would not carry guns.

Quakers had strong beliefs about God and followed strict customs. Children learned to sit quietly for hours at a time in the Quaker Meeting House where they worshiped. They were not allowed to dance, play music, or read storybooks.

The Declaration of Independence was adopted at the Philadelphia State House, later called Independence Hall. The Constitution of the United States was debated, written, and signed here.

From Student to Apprentice

Not all children went to school in colonial times, but Betsy went six days a week. At the Friends Public School, students practiced reading and writing. They also learned a trade. Sewing was Betsy's talent and her trade.

As a child, Betsy loved creating quilts. She also made samplers, or pieces of needlework with complex designs. Some historians say Betsy won many contests for her needlework. There is no doubt that Betsy was a skilled seamstress even in childhood.

Quakers wore simple clothes. Every day, Betsy put on a plain gray dress and white apron and cap.

The French and Indian War

During Betsy's childhood, Britain and its American colonies fought the French and Indian War (1754–1763) against France and its colony, Canada. Britain won the war, and Canada became a British colony.

The war was expensive for the British. To help pay the war's costs, the government planned to raise taxes in the American colonies. Most colonists felt they had already done enough to help Britain.

Betsy's schooling ended at age 12, when school was no longer thought necessary for girls. They soon would be wives and mothers. Betsy's father planned for his daughter to become an apprentice. An apprentice earns no money but learns a trade from a skilled worker.

Betsy worked for an upholsterer named John Webster. Today, we think of upholsterers as people who cover sofas and chairs with fabric. Upholsterers in colonial times did many other kinds of sewing jobs as well. They did fancy needlework for people's clothes and homes. Some even made flags.

Chapter Two

Betsy Ross, Seamstress

Betsy was not the only apprentice at John Webster's shop. John Ross also worked there, and he and Betsy became friends. The two shared a dream. Both wanted to have their own upholstery shop. It did not take long for Betsy and John to fall in love.

A Secret Wedding

John was not a Quaker, a fact that caused problems for the couple. Quakers did not like their members to marry someone who was not a Quaker. Betsy's parents did not approve of John as her choice for a husband. Betsy was pretty and had other Quaker men interested in marrying her. But Betsy had made up her mind.

Betsy married John Ross secretly. Her sister Sarah and Sarah's husband helped Betsy and John travel across the Delaware River. Betsy and John were married in a ceremony at Hugg's Tavern in New Jersey on November 4, 1773.

By His Excellency WILLIAM FRANKLIN, Esq.
Captain-General and Governor in Chief in and
over His Majesty's Province of *New-Jersey*, and
Territories thereon depending in *America*, &c.

++
To any *Protestant Minister, or Justice of the Peace.*
++

WHEREAS there is a mutual Purpose of Marriage between *John Ross of*
the City of Philadelphia
of the one Party, and *Elizabeth Griscomb of the same ph*
of the other Party ... when they have desired my Licence,
and have given Bond, upon Condition, that ... r of them have any lawful Let or
Impediment, Pre-Contract, Affinity or Consanguinity, to hinder their being joined in
the Holy Bands of Matrimony. These ... are to authorize and impower you to
join the said *John Ross* ... *Elizabeth Griscomb*
in the Holy Bands of Matrimony, ... pronounce Man and Wife.

GIVEN under my H... rogative Seal, at *Burlington* the *fourth*
Day of *Nov...* ... *foursixt*th Year of the Reign of our Sovereign Lord
GEORGE ... by the Grace of GOD, of Great-Britain, France and Ireland, King,
Defender of t... &c. Annoque Domini, One Thousand Seven Hundred and *Seventy three*

Entered in the Regis... erogative Office.

James Bonma

The name of New Jersey's governor is on Betsy and John Ross's wedding certificate. Governor William Franklin was Benjamin Franklin's son.

Chatelaine

Betsy wore a small silver clasp and chain called a chatelaine pinned at her waist. She hooked her scissors to it as well as a small steel ball to hold her pins. The chatelaine was a sign of Betsy's trade.

Betsy was happy to be Mrs. John Ross, but life was not easy. She moved in with John, and they opened their own upholstery shop. Philadelphia had many such shops, so business was slow. Then Betsy was forced to leave the Society of Friends for marrying outside her faith.

Clouds of War

Another problem was the growing unrest in the colonies. The colonists were talking about a revolt, or fight, against Britain. American colonists felt they had the right to decide their own taxes. The colonists did not have representation in the British government, or Parliament. For this reason, they believed Parliament was the wrong group to establish taxes.

Signs of war were everywhere. Many new flags were flying, and shop windows were filled with swords and guns. Men lined up in front of taverns to join militias. These groups of citizens were trained to fight in times of emergency.

Loyalists and Patriots

People were divided in their loyalties. Many people still felt King George III of Britain had a right to rule the colonies. These supporters were called Loyalists. Other citizens who were eager to fight to form a new nation were called Patriots. The Quakers tried to avoid trouble with the British. Some Quakers refused to fight but quietly supported the Patriots.

The British and the American Continental Army first clashed in the Battles of Lexington and Concord in Massachusetts. These battles started the Revolutionary War on April 19, 1775.

Betsy and John sided with the Patriots, but they felt the effects of war. Fabrics needed for their shop were now harder to find. John and Betsy worked every day but Sunday. At night, John helped the war effort. Betsy was left to clean and lock up their shop and take care of their home.

Betsy and John faced their problems. They moved their shop to Arch Street, hoping business would improve in the new location. Betsy no longer

Betsy and John Ross worshiped in this pew at Christ Church. It is still marked with their names. Today, a "Betsy Ross Flag" hangs by the pew.

12

Watch Where You Step!

A servant girl brought water to Betsy's door every morning so Betsy could wash. The girl also removed the chamber pot. This covered bowl was used as an indoor bathroom at night. The girl dumped the contents of the chamber pot in the outdoor toilet in the backyard. However, some people's servants just poured a pot's contents out the window. People had to be careful when walking the streets early in the morning.

was a Quaker, but she still worshiped with John. Their pew, or seat, at Christ Church was next to George Washington's pew. Washington sat there whenever he was in Philadelphia on a Sunday.

One night in January 1776, disaster struck. John was guarding an ammunition supply when it exploded. He was badly hurt. For days after the explosion, Betsy did all she could to help John, but he died. Betsy Ross became a widow just two years after her wedding.

The Betsy Ross House

The house at 239 Arch Street became known as the Betsy
Ross House. Betsy lived and worked here from 1773 to
1786. Legend says she made the first American flag here.
The house was restored as it might have looked in 1777
and is now open to the public. The photo on the right
shows how the house looks today.

A Widow in Troubled Times

Betsy was 24 years old when John died. She did not go back to John Webster's Upholstery Shop. Instead, Betsy carried on with her own business. Around this time, Betsy rented a room in a home at or near 239 Arch Street.

Betsy still went to Christ Church, where she had good friends, such as the Claypoole sisters. Their brother John once had wanted to marry Betsy. Now he was fighting in the war.

The war was not going well for the Americans at this time. No one knew when the fighting might reach Philadelphia, but people worried as the British marched closer.

Betsy sewed bed curtains and window hangings and did fancy sewing for people. But fancy needlework was not a good trade during war years. People worried about getting enough food, not about getting new curtains. It was hard to make a living, even though Betsy's skill was well known.

Choosing Independence

The move toward independence grew. More colonists wanted to manage their own affairs. They did not want to answer to Britain. Being an ocean

"Do not put such unlimited power into the hands of the Husbands. Remember all men would be tyrants [cruel rulers] if they could. If particular care and attention is not paid to the Ladies we are determined to foment [spur] a Rebellion, and will not hold ourselves bound by any Laws in which we have no voice, or Representation."

Abigail Adams, wife of John Adams, on the rights of women and the Declaration of Independence

away from Britain gave the colonists a feeling of independence.

The Continental Congress was America's unofficial government at the time. This group included Thomas Jefferson, Robert Morris, John Adams, Colonel George Ross, and other leaders. George Ross was an uncle of John Ross. The Congress held meetings at the Philadelphia State House. In early summer of 1776, Congress set up a committee to write a Declaration of Independence for the colonies.

The Continental Colors, America's first national flag, contained the British Union Jack. This symbol no longer was appropriate for the country after the Declaration of Independence. The nation needed a new flag.

Continental Colors

On January 1, 1776, the Continental Army was surrounding Boston. The British Army had taken over the city. George Washington flew the Continental Colors on a hill overlooking Boston. This flag later was called the Grand Union Flag. It featured a Union Jack, which was a British symbol. Some British mistook the raising of this flag as a sign that the Americans were giving up. However, Washington meant the flag to represent America's united forces. Because of the confusion, perhaps a new flag was needed.

Grand Union Flag 1776

Chapter Three

Birth of a Legend

According to Betsy's family, Colonel George Ross, Robert Morris, and General Washington came to Betsy's shop in the spring of 1776. The three men were a flag committee from Congress. Robert Morris owned a fleet of ships. He was eager for his ships to fly a real American flag. Colonel Ross knew that Betsy was very qualified to make the new flag. She was a true Patriot and could be trusted to sew the flag without a word to anyone.

Legend says that General Washington showed Betsy a rough drawing of a flag. The flag was square and had 13 stripes and 13 stars. Each star had six points.

According to Betsy's family, George Washington and two other men asked for Betsy's help in 1776. They wanted her to make the first copy of the flag now known as the Stars and Stripes.

Betsy Makes Improvements

Betsy is said to have had ideas for improving the flag's design. She recommended a rectangle rather than a square. This would help the flag fly better in the wind. She suggested stars with five points because they would be easier to make. Betsy then folded a piece of paper. By cutting one snip with her scissors, she made a five-pointed star. The men liked what they saw and used Betsy's ideas to change the drawing. They then asked her to sew a flag using the new design.

Betsy worked fast to make the flag. Her design was accepted quickly by Congress, which then ordered as many flags as Betsy could make. Her flags soon were flying from navy ships.

Turning Points

During the summer of 1776, people filled the city of Philadelphia. Rooms for rent were hard to find. Betsy was lucky to have found space upstairs in the house on Arch Street. Other people also slept in the Arch Street house, making it crowded. These people kept their belongings with them in case they had to flee quickly. No one knew if or when Philadelphia might come under attack.

Make a Five-Pointed Star Like Betsy's

You will need a thin sheet of paper. Use sheets that are 8 by 10 inches (22 by 25 centimeters). Fold and cut the paper as shown.

Step 1 • Fold the paper in half.

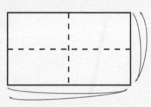

Step 2 • Keep paper folded in half. Then, fold and unfold it in half both ways. This forms creased center lines.

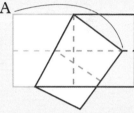

Step 3 • Bring corner (A) right until it meets the creased center line. Fold from the vertical creased line.

Step 4 • Bring corner (A) left until the edges meet, then make the fold.

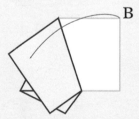

Step 5 • Bring corner (B) left and fold.

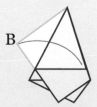

Step 6 • Bring corner (B) right until edges line up. Then fold.

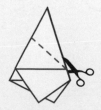

Step 7 • Cut on the angle as shown in the picture. Then unfold the small piece. Now, you should have a five-pointed star like Betsy's.

The war was going badly for the Continental Army. But on Christmas night, 1776, General Washington led a secret attack. He took his troops across the Delaware River. They surprised the enemy and won an important victory. American troops won again at Princeton, New Jersey, on January 2, 1777. Now there was hope. The victories meant that Philadelphia was safe for a time.

The new country needed many flags, and Betsy's needle was busy. Records show that she earned money by sewing naval flags, called ship's colors. She also sewed other materials such as tents and uniforms needed during the war.

A Flag for America

Records show that the Continental Congress made the new American flag design official on June 14, 1777. Congress passed a Flag Resolution, or official statement, that said: "Resolved. That the Flag of the United States be 13 stripes alternate red and white, that the Union be 13 stars white in a blue field representing a new constellation."

The Stars and Stripes

This flag with 13 stars and 13 stripes flew until 1795. In that year, Congress passed the Second Flag Act. Vermont and Kentucky had joined the Union in 1791 and 1792. The flag changed to 15 stars and 15 stripes.

In the resolution, Congress said nothing about the pattern for the stars. Flagmakers made their own designs. The most common patterns had the flag's stars in rows, squares, or circles. Various flags were used throughout the colonial period.

The day after the Flag Resolution passed, Betsy Ross married Joseph Ashburn. Joseph had been a suitor who lost Betsy to John Ross. Now he was a sea captain. Betsy had been Betsy Ross for only four years.

Chapter Four

War Surrounds Betsy

July 4, 1777, was the first anniversary of the birth of the United States. But the new nation was still fighting for freedom. The war came closer to Philadelphia, and many Patriots took flight. Many Quakers stayed and so did Betsy. Terror claimed Philadelphia while Betsy's new husband was at sea.

There was little good news. Washington urged Congress to leave Philadelphia in September. The British Army occupied Philadelphia in September 1777 and stayed nine long months. Enemy soldiers occupied every available room in the city. They ate the city's food, used up its fuel wood, and took its horses. Soldiers moved into the home where Betsy lived. Having the enemy in the house made conditions crowded and unpleasant.

The Liberty Bell

The British occupied Philadelphia from September 1777 to June 1778. Patriots removed all bells, including the Liberty Bell, from the city. If left, the bells would likely be melted down and used for cannon balls. Americans hid the Liberty Bell under the floorboards of the Zion Reformed Church in Allentown, Pennsylvania. After the British left Philadelphia, the Liberty Bell was returned to its place in the city.

Helping the Troops

Thousands of women followed the soldiers to their battles. Some loaded cartridges with gunpowder to save soldiers time on the battlefield. Some women brought bullets to soldiers. Some went to support husbands or to cook and wash laundry. Others, including Betsy, served as nurses to injured and sick soldiers. However, most women ran farms and businesses at home during the war's eight years.

The British finally marched from Philadelphia in June 1778, leaving their wreckage and rubbish behind. Life in the city improved. Betsy ran her shop. Then, on September 15, 1779, she and Joseph had a baby girl. They named her Lucilla and called her Zilla.

Endings

Another year of wartime went by, and it brought many changes. Betsy was expecting a second baby. Joseph went to sea again, and many months passed with no word from him. Baby Eliza was born in February 1781. Life was a struggle. The army's need for food, firewood, and supplies had brought terrible shortages and high prices to Philadelphia.

Women of the Revolution

Besides Betsy Ross, few women from the Revolution were written into history. Mary McCauley Hays (pictured below) is one legend of the war. She fetched water for her husband and his crew during the Battle of Monmouth (1778), earning her the name Molly Pitcher. When Mary's husband was wounded, she helped keep the guns firing.

Deborah Sampson dressed as a soldier and took the name "Robert Shurtleff." She fought in several battles before she became sick and doctors discovered her true identity. Deborah gave talks about her military service. She may have been the first female professional speaker in the United States.

PROVINCE OF QUÉBEC

The Great Lakes Region

MASSACHUSETTS
(District of Maine)

Nova Scotia

NEW HAMPSHIRE

Boston

MASSACHUSETTS

NEW YORK

RHODE ISLAND

PENNSYLVANIA

CONNECTICUT

Princeton

Philadelphia

NEW JERSEY

TERRITORY FROM BRITAIN

DELAWARE

Mississippi River

MARYLAND

VIRGINIA

Yorktown

NORTH
CAROLINA

SOUTH
CAROLINA

ATLANTIC
OCEAN

GEORGIA

SPANISH
FLORIDA

0 50 100 150 200

0 100 200 300

The United States in 1783

In October 1781, at Yorktown, Virginia, soldiers fought the last major battle of the Revolutionary War. The war was now over, and Betsy and her girls waited for Joseph to come home. But Joseph never came.

Betsy learned of her husband's death from their old friend, John Claypoole. Joseph had been on a trip to the West Indies to buy war supplies. He was captured by the British and sent to a prison in Britain. John Claypoole had been held captive in the same prison. Joseph died of an illness in March 1782 at the prison. Once again, war had taken Betsy's husband.

The American Revolution ended with the signing of the Treaty of Paris. This agreement took place in a quiet room in Paris, France, on September 3, 1783. Britain recognized the United States as a free and independent nation.

The treaty set the boundaries of the new nation. The United States now included most of the land from the Atlantic Ocean west to the Mississippi River. The northern border was set at the Great Lakes and along the borders of Québec and Nova Scotia, Canada.

Chapter Five

A Peaceful Life

Betsy married her old friend John Claypoole on May 8, 1783. Soon the two decided that they wanted to be Quakers again. Betsy and John joined a group of Quakers who had fought against the British. These Quakers no longer fit in with the rest of the Society of Friends. The Patriots formed their own group called the Society of Free Quakers.

Betsy was happy when John gave up life at sea. He worked with Betsy in her upholstery shop. Later, he worked at the U.S. Customs House in Philadelphia. Betsy had five more daughters with John. Their names were Clarissa Sidney, Susannah, Rachael, Jane, and Harriet. Two of Betsy's seven daughters died in childhood. They were Zilla, her firstborn, and baby Harriet.

This is the Free Quaker Meeting House where the Society of Free Quakers met. By 1834, only Betsy and one other Free Quaker were still attending the Meeting House. They agreed to close their beloved place of worship. With this, the Society of Free Quakers came to an end.

A Widow Once More

John Claypoole died in 1817 at age 64. Betsy and John had enjoyed 34 years of marriage, and Betsy never married again.

In 1827, Betsy left the business of making flags to her widowed daughter Clarissa. Betsy's granddaughter Sophia and her niece Margaret Boggs also worked in the shop. The shop stayed open until 1857.

After retiring, Betsy lived with her daughter Susannah Satterthwaite for a while. Later, she lived with her daughter Jane Canby. She enjoyed telling her story about the first American flag to her grandchildren. Betsy's eyesight failed in her

last years. But she sewed quilts and other items as long as she could.

Betsy lived to be 84 years old. She died at the Philadelphia home of her daughter Jane on January 30, 1836. Betsy first was buried in the graveyard of the Society of Free Quakers. In 1857, her remains were moved to Mount Moriah Cemetery. Betsy's remains were moved again in 1976, and her grave now is in the garden courtyard at the Betsy Ross House. She is buried next to her third husband, John Claypoole.

This is the Flag Room of the Betsy Ross House where Betsy lived and kept her shop.

Chapter Six

Fond Tale or True Story?

Betsy was not famous during her lifetime. Few people besides Betsy's family had heard her story of the first Stars and Stripes. That changed in 1870, when Betsy's grandson, William Canby, made her story public. He wrote it from his own memories of his grandmother Elizabeth Claypoole. He also interviewed his mother, who was Betsy's daughter. He talked with his elderly aunts, Betsy's sisters. Then he presented the story of the flag to the Historical Society of Pennsylvania.

After Canby's speech, the Betsy Ross story quickly spread. In 1876, the country celebrated its 100th year of independence. It was a time when Americans were looking for heroes. By 1900, the story had become a part of the American memory. Truth or tale, the story became a legend.

Betsy may have used
these scissors when
making the flag.

If Not Betsy, Then Who?

Research suggests that Francis Hopkinson, a member of the Continental Congress, designed the first Stars and Stripes. Some experts say Betsy Ross probably sewed one early flag. She likely sewed the first Stars and Stripes for the naval forces defending Philadelphia in 1777.

Is There Proof?

Millions of students have been taught that Betsy Ross made the first Stars and Stripes for George Washington. But flags were not mentioned in reports from the time. The known facts leave room for doubt. For example, no known sources refer to a flag committee, and no known sources mention the adoption of any flag by Congress before 1777. There is no known proof that Betsy Ross and George Washington even knew each other.

The first public knowledge of Betsy's role came 94 years after the events in question. Experts say this is strange. They wonder if William Canby remembered Betsy's stories correctly. After all, he was just a boy of 11 when his Grandmother Betsy died. Canby gathered affidavits, or written

statements, from others such as Betsy's daughter, niece, and granddaughter. These people said they had heard the story from Betsy Ross's lips.

Other researchers favor the Betsy Ross legend and have their own reasons to do so. Congressional records and Washington's own letters help verify Betsy's story. They place Washington in Philadelphia from late May to early June of 1776, around the time he was supposed to have met with Betsy.

Proof exists that Betsy did make flags for Pennsylvania. A note dated May 29, 1777, from the State Navy Board says payment was made to Elizabeth Ross for making ship's colors. However, there is no note of the specific flags for which she was paid.

The American flag flew 24 hours a day at Betsy's grave in Mount Moriah Cemetery.

Remembering Betsy

Betsy Ross was indeed a loyal Patriot. She lost two husbands to the war. She cared for sick and wounded soldiers when the British took over Philadelphia. She sewed needed materials for the army and made many flags for land and sea.

A Bridge to Honor Betsy

A major Philadelphia bridge is named in honor of Betsy Ross. The bridge opened April 30, 1976. It is the first bridge in the United States to be named after a woman.

Did You Know?

Betsy Ross is only one of two real people from history featured as the head of a Pez candy dispenser.

Betsy's story is about courage in the time of danger. It is about keeping hope during the dark days of war. It is also about dedication to a cause and staying with a goal.

Betsy had great energy and courage. She was a devoted wife and mother and a modern woman for her time. Betsy did not simply go along with the roles set by her Quaker family or American society. She thought for herself, followed her dreams, and ran her own business.

Betsy Ross was one of the few women from her time to be written into history. The truth about the first Stars and Stripes may never fully be known. But the life of Betsy Ross is worth knowing about, and the legend of Betsy Ross is likely here to stay.

TIMELINE

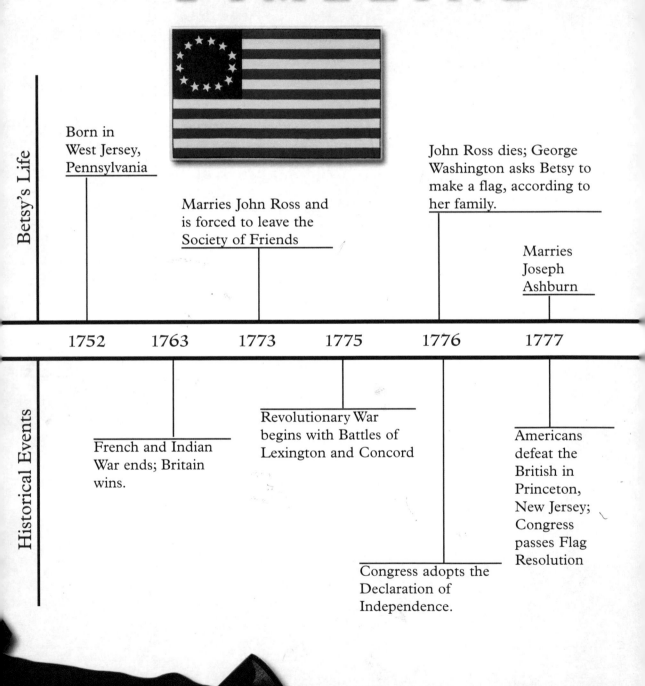

Betsy's Life

Born in West Jersey, Pennsylvania

Marries John Ross and is forced to leave the Society of Friends

John Ross dies; George Washington asks Betsy to make a flag, according to her family.

Marries Joseph Ashburn

1752   1763   1773   1775   1776   1777

Historical Events

French and Indian War ends; Britain wins.

Revolutionary War begins with Battles of Lexington and Concord

Congress adopts the Declaration of Independence.

Americans defeat the British in Princeton, New Jersey; Congress passes Flag Resolution

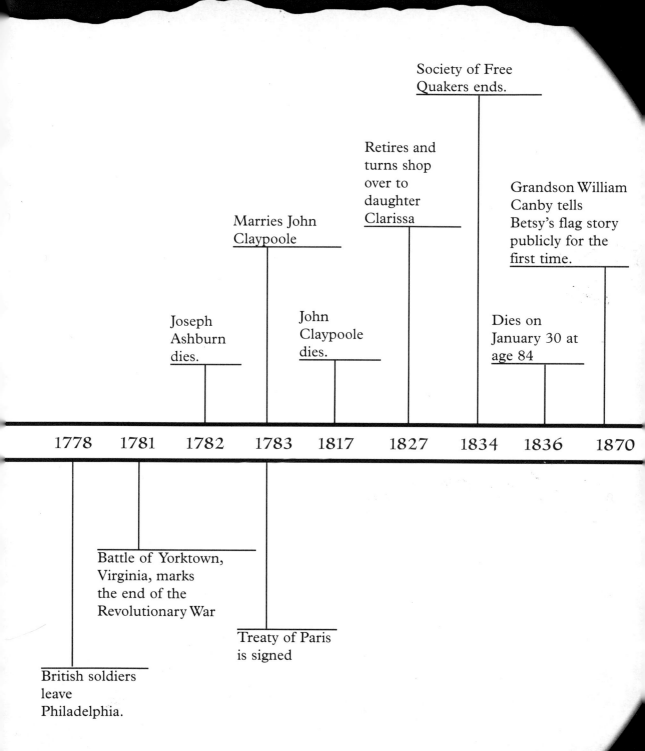

Society of Free
Quakers ends.

Retires and
turns shop
over to
daughter
Clarissa

Grandson William
Canby tells
Betsy's flag story
publicly for the
first time.

Marries John
Claypoole

Joseph
Ashburn
dies.

John
Claypoole
dies.

Dies on
January 30 at
age 84

1778   1781   1782   1783   1817   1827   1834   1836   1870

Battle of Yorktown,
Virginia, marks
the end of the
Revolutionary War

Treaty of Paris
is signed

British soldiers
leave
Philadelphia.

Glossary

ammunition (am-yuh-NISH-uhn)—a supply of gunpowder, musket balls, or bullets to use in guns

apprentice (uh-PREN-tiss)—a person who works without pay to learn a trade or art from a skilled person

chatelaine (SHA-tuhl-ayn)—a hook and chain pinned to a garment; Betsy Ross wore a chatelaine with a scissors and pin ball attached as a sign of her trade.

colony (KOL-uh-nee)—an area of land and water settled and governed by a distant country

Free Quaker (FREE KWAY-kur)—a Quaker who supported and may even have fought in the Revolutionary War

Loyalist (LOI-uh-list)—a colonist loyal to King George III and Britain during the Revolutionary War; Loyalists, also called Tories, felt Britain had a right to rule the colonies.

militia (muh-LISH-uh)—a group of citizens who are trained to fight but serve only in times of emergency

Patriot (PAY-tree-uht)—a colonist loyal to America during the Revolutionary War; Patriots wanted to form a free, new nation independent of Britain.

Quaker (KWAY-kur)—a member of the religious group known as the Society of Friends

resolution (rez-uh-LOO-shuhn)—a formal statement of a decision

upholstery (uhp-HOHL-stur-ee)—fabric used to make furniture coverings

widow (WID-oh)—a woman whose husband has died

For Further Reading

Bennett, William J., ed. *Our Country's Founders: A Book of Advice for Young People.* New York: Simon & Schuster Books for Young Readers, 1998.

Miller, Susan Martins. *Betsy Ross: American Patriot.* Revolutionary War Leaders. Philadelphia: Chelsea House, 2000.

Roop, Connie, and Peter Roop. *Betsy Ross.* In Their Own Words. New York: Scholastic Reference, 2001.

St. George, Judith. *Betsy Ross: Patriot of Philadelphia.* New York: Henry Holt, 1997.

Todd, Anne. *The Revolutionary War.* America Goes to War. Mankato, Minn.: Capstone Books, 2001.

Places of Interest

Betsy Ross House
239 Arch Street
Philadelphia, PA 19106
Betsy is now buried on the
grounds of her home and shop.

Christ Church
Second and Market Streets
Philadelphia, PA 19106
Here, Betsy and John Ross
attended church along with
George Washington.

Free Quaker Meeting House
Arch Street between Fifth and
Sixth Streets
Philadelphia, PA 19106
The building where Betsy
worshiped as a member of
the Society of Free Quakers.

**Independence National
Historical Park**
Third and Chestnut Streets
Philadelphia, PA 19106
Includes Independence Hall
where Betsy's father helped
build the bell tower.

Internet Sites

The American Flag Page
http://userpages.aug.com/haywire/main.html
Provides historical and current information on the U.S. flag.

Betsy Ross Homepage
http://www.ushistory.org/betsy/index.html
Includes interesting flag facts, a picture gallery of historical American flags, and the paper Betsy's grandson read to the Historical Society of Pennsylvania.

The Betsy Ross House
http://www.ushistory.org/betsy/flaghome.html
Lets you take a virtual tour of the house on Arch Street.

Pennsylvania Historical and Museum Commission
http://www.phmc.state.pa.us
Contains information on Pennsylvania's historical events.

Index